Something Worth Giving a Thought!!
あ〜気づきさえすれば！！

菅野 末喜

気づき
Have You Ever Thought?

人生なるようになる。

Life will take its course naturally.

でも

やった様にしか

ならないのも事実。

However,

You will have to direct the life to take the path you want.

どうなりたい？

Want something to happen?

うん！

Yup!

じゃあ、やろうよ！！

Well, then let's try for it!!

気づき
Have You Ever Thought?

毎日の些細なことは
深く考えないで
無意識に選択し、
行動する。

We take decisions unconsciously
And act accordingly
Without pondering on the
Trivial things in daily life.

人生は
殆んど小さな事の
積み重ねの集大成。

Life is nothing but the compilation of
such small things.

ちょっと意識して過ごすのも
悪くない！！！

Then why not try to be more conscious about those
things?

気づき
Have You Ever Thought?

やりたい事がいっぱいあると、

時間の使い方が上手くなる。

When there's a good chunk of things

that you want to do,

managing time doesn't seem to be difficult!

一日が充実する！！！

And your whole day is enriched!

やらねばならない事を、

やりたい事に……☆

Just a slight difference in the perception,

from duty to desire…☆

気づき
Have You Ever Thought?

時間に追いかけられるのは

苦しい……

Being chased by the time is agonising

時間を追いかけるのは

楽しい……

While, chasing time is fun!!...

マイペースでつかまえて、

マイペースで使う。

Let's grab the time at our own pace

And use it at our own whim

それが、それぞれの

人生の中味

……だと思う。

Well, I guess this is the essence of one's 1

自分の生き方は

自分できめられる

To live life in one's own way!

気づき
Have You Ever Thought?

うまず

たゆまず

コツコツと

目標にむかって

一直線！！！

Hang in there and run

Straight towards the goal!!!

今日もだれかに

自分のバトンを渡せると

いいな！！

I wish I will get somebody today

to pass on my baton!!

気づき
Have You Ever Thought?

何でもくせになると

面白い★★★

We develop habit of almost anything.

Interesting, isn't it?

せっかくだから

よいくせを身につけよう！

Then why not try get habitual to some good things?

早寝・早起き・

プラス思考で！！！

Like getting up and going to bed early, thinking positively!!!

気づき
Have You Ever Thought?

人は自分の鏡

いい思いをいただけるのも

悪い思いをするのも

それは自分がそうしているから

People around you are a mirror.

Some are nice to you, Some are mean to you.

It's because you are doing the same thing to them.

気づき
Have You Ever Thought?

朝の時間が大切

Morning time is very important.

身なりと心を

整えていると

いい事はやってくる

Because it is the time to get prepared from inside and outside to welcome the good things coming along in our way!

ラッキーな事は

準備できている人に

めぐってくると……

思いたい。

It is believed that the good fortune comes around the people who are prepared for it.

気づき
Have You Ever Thought?

物事を

The things proceed smoothly in most of the cases,

上手く進めて行く上では

相手の都合を 50%

自分の都合も 50%と、

考えて行動すると

たいていは上手く行く！！

if you give equal importance to your partner's

comfort

and convenience as your own.

……のでは？

Have you noticed this?

気づき
Have You Ever Thought?

足りてることを

知ることは

幸福への第一歩。

To get aware of what is enough for life is the first step towards happiness.

これがなかなか

難しい！が……

Though, it's a little bit difficult...

ありがたいなぁ～と

思える気持ちが

あれば常に

心は大満足♥

Being grateful to everything in life will give your mind a sustained satisfaction!

気づき
Have You Ever Thought?

よろこびは
友と分かちあうと
倍になり
悲しみは和らぐ

A joy gets double while the edges of sorrow get cut off, when shared with friends.

一生の中で、そんな
心許せる友が
どれだけできるか……

How many such trustworthy friends you make in your whole life …

人生に成功するとは
そういう事だと思う

I think it's the key to success!

気づき
Have You Ever Thought?

平凡な日常のいちにちが

実は幸せな日なんだ……

Every ordinary day is a blessing

それに気がつき

有難いと思って過ごす

その日が特別

And the day you realize it and be grateful to that
blessing is the special one.

気づき
Have You Ever Thought?

ほっとしたり
がっかりしたり
嬉しかったり
悲しかったり
思えば１日１年
この繰り返し。

Every single day is an emotional roller coaster riding you through the solace, dismay, bliss, grief repeatedly.

がっかりした時に
次があるさと
考えればほっとする。

When dismayed, thinking about the next step of this ride will make you feel relieved.

なんだ！！
結局は同じ事
考え方次第だね。

After all everything is based on your perception.

気づき
Have You Ever Thought?

『いつか、きっと……』

と、思いながら、

今、この時に、

どう過ごしているのかな？

You hope for something to happen "someday surely in Future" and keep waiting for it in present.

『いつか、きっと……』

は、先にあるのではなく、

今にあるのだ。

Live life in this very moment, rather waiting for future.

気づき
Have You Ever Thought?

皆さんは、どんな人が好き？

What kind of person you like?

前向きな人

A positive person

明るく元気な人

A bright and energetic person

言い訳をしない人

A person who does not give excuses

約束を守る人

A promise keeping person

ウラ・オモテがない人

・・・・

An honest person

自分の好きな人を

目指せば

間違いない！！！

You won't get wrong if you aim for your favourite person!!!

気づき
Have You Ever Thought?

昨日の成功や失敗は

過ぎ去ったこと。

Your yesterday's achievements or failures

is a part of past.

明日はまだやってこない。

And the tomorrow is yet to come!

だからこそ

今日のこの1日に

集中していこう！

So, just concentrate on today!

今日がすべて。

All you have is just today.

気づき
Have You Ever Thought?

時間はだれにでも平等にやってくる。
お金のように価値に差はない。

Every person gets the equal time unlike money with different denominations.

自分の使い方で
価値が決まる。

What decides the value of time is nothing but the way you use it.

これは間違いなく
嬉しい事……だと思う。

And I feel, it's surely a good thing!

気づき
Have You Ever Thought?

やる気と元気はどこから来る？

……それはねっ♪

どこから来るか

見た人はいないんですが……

From where does one get the motivation and energy?

Ohhh...

There is no one who saw it coming along the way...

But...

……自分が幸せだ

と感じた時に

元気がでるんだよ〜♬

When you feel happy and contented,

energy comes out. ♬

やる気が出るのは

喜んでくれる人が

身近にいる時なんだよ〜♪

And the motivation comes out when you have someone

happy with your efforts...

どちらも気持ちしだいです。

Both depend on feelings.

気づき
Have You Ever Thought?

苦あれば、楽あり

If there is a pain, there will be comfort also.

楽あれば、苦あり

If there is a comfort, there will be pain in a while.

苦を好きになれば

楽もすぐにやってくる。

Once you get used to with the pain

the comfort will also come to you.

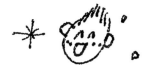

気づき
Have You Ever Thought?

肉体の
新陳代謝は衰えても
心の代謝は
自分でできる。

The metabolism of body will get weaker and weaker,
but you can always restore your young spirit of mind!

何かにワクワクしよう！！
それがきっと
心を若返らせるぞ！！

Feel the excitement towards anything and everything!
That will rejuvenate your mind!

気づき
Have You Ever Thought?

見たいものがある

There are things we want to see!

知りたい事がある

There are things we want to know about!

伝えたい事がある

There are things we want to express!

行きたい所がある

There are places we want to go!

やってみたい事がある

There are things we want to try!

少しずつそれを

かなえていく。

Let's try to fulfil these wishes one by one....

そんな１日１日の

積み重ねを

目指して……

Let's aim at having more and more such days of dream accomplishments!!

気づき
Have You Ever Thought?

良いことも、悪いことも
毎日の積み重ねが
1年・2年……
10年後の自分

Our good and bad deeds today
will contribute to our identity after say 1,2....10 years

自分にとってもいい事が
人にとってもいい事
この積み重ねが
元気の源。

What we think good for us is also good for other people
and such good acts provide the good energy.

元気・やる気・は
お金を出さなくて
も手に入る

One doesn't need money to get the energy, spirit, motivation...

気づき
Have You Ever Thought?

運が良い……

悪い……

これは偶然の産物でしょうか？

Is getting good or bad fortune mere a coincidence?

ひたむきに取り組む姿勢が

良い運を呼ぶのでは？

……そう信じたい……

それが全て。

Don't you think that the luck favour those who have the

passionate devotion?

In the end, that's all we have to believe.

気づき
Have You Ever Thought?

近頃思う……
全てがうまくいったと思う日
よりも
少し悔いが残ったほうがいい
明日は悔いが残らぬよう
頑張れるから……

Lately I have been feeling,
ending a day with a pinch of regret is
better than with a satisfaction of everything went perfect.
Because, it will induce you to strive to overcome that regret.

気づき
Have You Ever Thought?

何かいやな事が
When something bad
自分に起こったら
happens,
それは自分を
活気付けてくれる
ビタミン剤だと思おう！
Accept it like a vitamin tablet, which makes us strong.
昔から
良薬は口に苦し
というではないか……
As it is been said;
Good medicines are bitter in taste!

気づき
Have You Ever Thought?

失ってみて初めて気づく。

失ったものの大切さを。

We realise the importance of things after losing them.

だから今ある事を

当たり前に思わないで

Therefore, do not take things you have

for granted

有り難いと思えば

If you are grateful for the things you have got,

大切に出来る

cherish them!!

気づき
Have You Ever Thought?

良い事も、悪い事も

それがず〜っと

続く事はない

Good fortune or bad fortune, either won't last forever...

またたくまに

過ぎ去っていく

些細な事

何事にもとらわれないで

今に集中！

Don't get distracted by such things that change in the twinkling

of the eye.

Instead focus on your present!

気づき
Have You Ever Thought?

何才になっても

Regardless of the age,

がむしゃらに取り組める

何かを持ってる事は

幸せの極み！！！

having the attitude of handling things a bit recklessly

is the extremity of happiness.

若さはそんな気もちから

生まれるのでは？

This attitude is the source of the young spirit, isn't it?

気づき
Have You Ever Thought?

●使わなくても減って

いくもの時間！

……補充出来ない

The thing that diminishes even if not used is the time.

Moreover, it is not replenishable.

●使って減るもの

お金と物！！

……補充出来るとは

限らない。

The things that diminish as much as you use them are

money and

commodities.

●使えば増えるもの

考え方！！！

いつでもどこでも

補充できる

いいねっ

But there exist a thing which increases by using more and more and which can be replenished anywhere anytime.

That is your

thinking ability!

気づき
Have You Ever Thought?

今、ここ、この一瞬

すべては

過ぎ去っていくもの

This moment, this ambience

Everything will disappear once...

感動は

次の行動に

つながる

心に残る感動を

いっぱい

残そうよ！！！

Only the thing which will remain is the heartfelt emotions......

So, let us feel everything by heart and fill our minds with the

feelings, those that will remain forever....

気づき
Have You Ever Thought?

しあわせは、
必ずしも物質の豊かさだけが
もたらすものではないと思う
Happiness is not something which can be brought by the material wealth!!!
当り前に見てたり
受けとめていると
日常に大きな喜びがあるのに
気づかない。
If we do not appreciate anything and take everything for granted, we may
miss to celebrate small joys in daily life.
それに気づかないのは
もったいない！！！
もったいないのは
物に対してだけでは
ないんだネ！

Being unaware of those joys is worthless!!!
Worthless are not always objects!!

気づき
Have You Ever Thought?

365日の日常の中に
小さな喜びは、いっぱいある。
豊かな感性を持ち続け
それをキャッチしていく事が
幸せへの道

Little pleasures lie in every day of the whole year.
Be sensitive towards them... Feel and enjoy those moments ...
It is the way to happiness...

気づき
Have You Ever Thought?

◇　◇　◇

若さを保つ為には
身心を鍛えること！！！
と、あった。
肉体の鍛錬には
限界があるが
脳の鍛錬には
限界がないらしい。
単純な感動も
脳の若さの源らしい。
単純だネ！

Physical and mental workout is necessary to stay young.

There is a limit to train your body but not for your mind.

Even simple sensations can be the source of youthfulness
to the mind.

Isn't it simple!

気づき
Have You Ever Thought?

年は重ねても

心まで老いなくても

よいのでは？

毎日なにかに感動し

何か人の為になる事をし、

常に好奇心を持って過ごし

感動・生き甲斐・好奇心

これさえあれば

いつでも青春♪

Isn't it good to get old but remain young at heart?
Feel everything, have the passion for doing something for someone and have the curiosity towards the unknown.
Having passion, purpose, and curiosity is the key to remain
young at any age!

気づき
Have You Ever Thought?

想像は行動の原点かも
10年後の自分を
ではなく1年後の自分を
どうなっていたいか
想像してみると……
今自分がやるべき事が
みえてくる

Imagination can stimulate the action!
Rather than thinking 10 years ahead,
imagine yourself a year later.
You will get to see what you have to do now.

気づき
Have You Ever Thought?

真の気づきは
行動につながる
気づきのある毎日が
人生をワクワク
豊かにする
気づきの素は
素直さにあり！！！

True realization leads to the action.
Every day lived with awareness makes life exciting.
And the origin of awareness is in the acceptance!!

気づき
Have You Ever Thought?

あれこれ
思い描いてても
実行していかなければ
はじまらない
結果はどうあれ
人は行動した分
だけしか成長
出来ないのでは？

You won't achieve anything by just visualizing about it.
Nothing will happen unless any action is taken.
Whatever will be the outcome,
but you will grow more and more as you take the efforts.
Don't think so?

気づき
Have You Ever Thought?

◇

何事も
やらねばならない気持ちを
やりたい気持ちに
リセットすると
楽しくはかどる！！！

All you have to do
is change your attitude
from having to do something
to willing to do something!
And things will proceed smoothly for you!!

気づき
Have You Ever Thought?

おひとつ、どうぞ……
だれかと分かち合えば
喜びも倍になる！！！
分かち合えるものを
もっと持てるように
努力しよっと！！！

Here, have one more!
Happiness gets doubled
when you share something with someone!!
So
just try hard
to get more and more of something
that you can share!!!!

気づき
Have You Ever Thought?
◇ ◇ ◇

人生はシンプルがいい！！

寝る！

働く！

遊ぶ！（楽しむ）

学ぶ！

24 時間を

バランス良く使う！！！

Simple living is always better!!

Sleep, work, learn, enjoy...

Have a balanced day!

気づき
Have You Ever Thought?

何に喜びを感じるかは
人それぞれ
与えてもらえる喜びよりも
喜こんでもらえるほうが
はるかに嬉しい。
今年も良かった〜の
貯金を！！！

It differs from person to person what makes them happy.
Getting the satisfaction by sprinkling happiness in others life is way more blissful than having showers of joy in our own life.
Have the capital of such happy days!!

気づき
Have You Ever Thought?

旅をして気がついた。
持っていく荷物は
最小限が良い。
人生も同じだと
思う。
身軽な程フットワークが
軽くなり楽しめる！！

Life is an expedition. As I travelled, it dawned on me
that the journey towards eternal bliss becomes easy
when one's not weighed down.
The stroll of life will rejuvenate you
if you have less burden with you.

気づき
Have You Ever Thought?

未来は分からない
でも、自分の未来は
今日の
この一歩の積み重ね
今日できることを精一杯。
それが
自分の未来を確実にする

No one knows what's in store for us.

Every step we take in present will lead to our future.

So, the only way to secure a better tomorrow is

to take our utmost efforts today.

気づき
Have You Ever Thought?

青春って？……
何かをしたいと思う
強い意志
やわらかな感性
つきぬ想像力
一途な冒険心
易きに流されぬ
心がけ
だれでも持てる
こんな気持ち
自分次第でいくつに
なっても青春時代

Have you ever thought what youth exactly is?
It's a strong intention to achieve something, a sensibility,
an endless imaginative
power.
an earnest adventurous spirit, a steady struggle……
Anyway having this young spirit will stay young at any
age!

気づき
Have You Ever Thought?

物事はすべて
考え方次第。
裏と表・太陽と月、
陰と陽、
日が昇れば、
日は沈む。
どっちを見るかで
心も体も温まる。

Things totally depend on the way of thinking.
A coin always has two faces, like back and front,
sun and moon, positive and negative. There are sunrises
and sunsets as well.
It will make you feel warm by seeing any of them!!

気づき
Have You Ever Thought?

仕事も学業も
家事・労働も、
同じやるなら
楽しくやろう！！！

Enjoy everything in your life;
Whether it's your work, studies, household chores or labour

出来ることを、
精一杯！！！
結果は2の次！！！

Just do what you can do
with all your might!!
The outcome
is secondary!!

気づき
Have You Ever Thought?

好きな事があるのは
それだけで幸せ。

Happiness is having something
you like the most!

好きな事

好きな物

好きな人

を

いっぱい作って

幸せ貯金を

していこう！！！！

Let's have more of everything in life;
Our favourite hobbies, people, things....
And let's have a good treasure of happy moments!!

気づき
Have You Ever Thought?

１日１回は
空を見上げよう。
心の翼を広げ
思いっきり上へ上へと
行ってみよう！
Let's look at the sky
once a day...
Spread out the wings of heart
and let's go on the top!!
広くて髙い空から
自分を見つめると
悲しいことも
嬉しいことも
そんなに違いはなく
ただ、ただ、生きていることを
大きな喜びを感じるよ。
After looking at ourselves
from the high blue sky,
we will not find much difference between
our tiny sorrows and joys...
We will only feel blessed and happy to be alive!!!!

気づき
Have You Ever Thought?

この一年

元気で

健康で

よかった〜♥

うれしい〜

It was a healthy and happy year and I'm satisfied with this.

全てに感謝を。

ありがとう。

I am really very grateful for such a great year.

こんな1年の積み重ねが

最高！！

It would be simply great to have many more such years as this!!

幸か不幸かは考え方次第！！
Happiness or unhappiness depend upon our way of thinking!!
人生は短い！不平不満を言ったり、
競争したり、怒ったり、いさかいを
してる時間はない。
Life is short; hence we have no time for complaints,
Competition, anger or argument.
あるがままを受け入れ今、この
一瞬一瞬を大切に！！
Just accept the things as they are and cherish each and every moment of life!!!

Positive thinking leads you to happiness.

Something Worth
Giving a Thought!!

あ～気づきさえすれば！！

2018 年 8 月 30 日　初版第 1 刷発行

著　者　菅野 末喜
発行所　ブイツーソリューション
　　　　〒 466-0848 名古屋市昭和区長戸町 4-40
　　　　電話 052-799-7391　　Fax 052-799-7984
発売元　星雲社
　　　　〒 112-0005 東京都文京区水道 1-3-30
　　　　電話 03-3868-3275　　Fax 03-3868-6588
印刷所　藤原印刷
ISBN 978-4-434-24979-2
©Maki Sugano 2018 Printed in Japan
万一、落丁乱丁のある場合は送料当社負担でお取替えいたします。
ブイツーソリューション宛にお送りください。